MISSIONS: GOD'S OWN PROJECT

MISSIONS: GOD'S OWN PROJECT

ADEWUNMI MAKANJUOLA

MISSIONS: GOD'S OWN PROJECT
Copyright © 2025 by Adewunmi Makanjuola

All rights reserved. Neither this publication nor any part of this publication may be reproduced or transmitted in any form or by any means, electronic or mechanical, including photocopying, recording or any information storage and retrieval system, without permission in writing from the author.

Scripture quotations taken from the (NASB®) New American Standard Bible®, Copyright © 1960, 1971, 1977, 1995, 2020 by The Lockman Foundation. Used by permission. All rights reserved. lockman.org. Scripture quotations marked (KJV) taken from the Holy Bible, King James Version, which is in the public domain. Scripture marked (NKJV) taken from the New King James Version®. Copyright © 1982 by Thomas Nelson. Used by permission. All rights reserved. Scripture quotations marked (NIV) are taken from the Holy Bible, New International Version®, NIV®. Copyright © 1973, 1978, 1984, 2011 by Biblica, Inc.™ Used by permission of Zondervan. All rights reserved worldwide. www.zondervan.com The "NIV" and "New International Version" are trademarks registered in the United States Patent and Trademark Office by Biblica, Inc.™

ISBN: 978-1-4866-2719-6
eBook ISBN: 978-1-4866-2720-2

Word Alive Press
119 De Baets Street Winnipeg, MB R2J 3R9
www.wordalivepress.ca

Cataloguing in Publication information can be obtained from Library and Archives Canada.

This book is dedicated to
Uncle Bayo Famonure,
the man
from whose mouth
I first ever heard about missions.
He will live long.

CONTENTS

FOREWORD	ix
ACKNOWLEDGEMENTS	xi
PREFACE	xiii
INTRODUCTION	xv
CHAPTER ONE: WHAT IS MISSIONS?	1
CHAPTER TWO: GOD'S INTENTION SCUTTLED?	5
CHAPTER THREE: THE COMING OF THE BLESSING	15
CHAPTER FOUR: ALL THE FAMILIES OF THE EARTH	19
CHAPTER FIVE: A CHRISTIAN, AN EVANGELIST	27
CHAPTER SIX: GO YE…	33
CHAPTER SEVEN: DISCIPLES SCATTERED	39
CHAPTER EIGHT: PERPETRATING THE BLESSING	43
CHAPTER NINE: PAUL THE MISSIONARY	51
CHAPTER TEN: GOD'S PROVIDENCE	63
CHAPTER ELEVEN: HOW WEALTHY ARE YOU?	67
CONCLUSION	73
ABOUT THE AUTHOR	75

FOREWORD

The concept of missions isn't new in our world. However, it didn't engage the attention of Africans until very recently. Missions, as we knew it, was always about spreading the gospel from the West to the rest of the world.

But the paradigm has shifted, and it has done so immensely. The old concept of missions was not what God had in mind. Either due to wrong teachings or a lack of understanding, these wrong concepts were taught and accepted for decades.

That is why this book has been written.

Right from the foundation of the world, God had missions in mind. He is actually a missionary God. As the author writes, missions has featured in God's working and thinking throughout the Bible. Thank God that today we are reverting to His original purpose.

Many in Africa, Asia, and Latin America have now joined the West in going out into the world as missionaries. In fact, the number of non-Western missionaries now far exceeds the number of Western missionaries. This is a good development. It means that all the years of toil by the West have not been in vein.

Sadly, however, there are people in our world who still have not heard of Jesus Christ, who came, died, and rose again two thousand years ago. Sadder still is the fact that some regions that were once covered by the gospel of Jesus have since plunged back into utter darkness. Countries like Great Britain, whose people pioneered missionary work, are now in dire need of missionaries themselves.

We can lament with the prophet Jeremiah, who wrote, *"How dark the gold has become! How the pure gold has changed!"* (Lamentations 4:1)

This book's copious references to the Bible, its incisive and thorough analysis of God's commands, and the author's articulate expression of the legal mind make the message easy to understand. *Missions: God's Own Project* represents a great leap towards mobilizing the body of Jesus Christ for the work the Master died for us to carry out. May the name of the Lord be glorified. Amen!

Rev. Canon Bayo Famonure

ACKNOWLEDGEMENTS

I give glory to God for His grace and the extensive patience He expended on me to write this book.

I affectionately acknowledge Uncle Bayo Famonure, the father of African missions; Rev. Dr. Mike Bamidele, presiding bishop of Victory Life Ministries International in Ilesa, Nigeria; and Pastor Mark Hughes of the Church of the Rock in Winnipeg, Manitoba for their precious inputs in my Christian journey.

I also acknowledge Autie Naomi Famonure of Agape Missions in Gana Ropp, near Jos, Nigeria; Rev. Mary Titi Bamidele of Victory Life Ministries in Ilesa; Rev. Olusola Ayodele Areogun of the Dream Centre in Osogbo; Rev. Odun Orioke of Christ Life Church in Ile-Ife; Mama Ruth Elton of Coming Kingdom Outreach in Ilesa; Pastor John Ladega of Kingdom Gospel Mission in Ilesa; Rev. Fred Adigun of FOLMO Missions in Ibadan; and Rev. Andrew Abah of Grace Foundation Inland Missions in Jos, as well as several other ministerial leaders and friends who cannot be mentioned here for space. Their diverse support and encouragement over the years have contributed to the making of this book. May the Lord bless and reward you all.

I heartily appreciate my dear wife, Adetayo, who has always been with me. Not only did she accompany me on all my mission trips, but her thoughts and ideas have always been apt. May God will surely bless her.

Lastly, I acknowledge my lovely children—Obalolu, Joshua and Nini-Peace—for their godly comportment and prayers. You are blessed of the Lord.

PREFACE

The writing of this book has been borne out of a deep-seated desire in my heart to show the whole world the conviction which I came to through the study of the Holy Bible. Through understanding what it truly means to live as a Christian, I have learned that missions has the main outlook of the almighty God, creator of heaven and earth, since before the foundations of the earth.

Throughout the Bible days, missions have featured in God's thoughts and workings. In the present dispensation, they have remained centre stage in importance to all aspects of sincere Christian endeavour. In fact, it is going to be the crucial climax of it all!

In this book, I will demonstrate that engaging in missions and missionary activities is crucial and imperative for all Christians in these last days.

INTRODUCTION

The *Bible* remains the bestselling book of all time. It is unique in many ways, including in terms of its message, its object, thrust, volume, characters, accuracy, correlation, correctness, currentness, infallibility, sweetness, and power. It remains unbeatable in its quality.

For now, however, we are interested mainly in its style.

Writers adopt different styles to pass along their message. Some may choose to disclose their subject right from the beginning, while others choose to leave the reader in suspense until the tail end. Some books contain hidden messages right in the middle of the text. In other books, the message could be brought together from different parts entirely.

This final style is the one in which the Bible is written. The reader of the Bible cannot read any one part and conclude that he has learned everything about any given topic. To pick the full gist of any subject, like missions, please be ready to search the entire Bible.

A careful reading of the various parts of the Bible points to a certain end: the emergence of Jesus Christ as the blessing of God to the entire world. The completion of this work of redemption necessitated His marching orders for all Christians to *go into all the world* and teach the gospel for the redemption of the entire world which He had come to save. The Christian mission is no less than total obedience to that command, as demonstrated in the book of Acts and culminating in Revelation. This, in summary, is the New Testament.

The question then is why did Jesus Christ come to the world? This gets to the issue of sin. Notice that the issue of sin came up almost immediately after the creation and blessing of man by God. The sin of Adam brought about the fall, including curse, spoilage, displacement, destruction, deprivation, delusion, hunger, thirst, depression, disease, and loss. And sin still brings about all these misfortunes today. So sin was a crucial matter for God to settle.

I choose to refer to the emergence of sin as the prologue to the Bible story. Because of it, humanity needed a cure—and that redemption came through a Messiah. The world needed to be reached and redeemed by God, who sent and appointed servants to lead the way, prophets to foretell the coming of the Messiah and prepare the way for Him.

The Bible reveals that rather than resolve the issue, all of the above interventions led to a worsening of the problems created by mankind's sin in their relationship with God. The world is still lost today, hence the necessity of Christian missions.

I shall in this book attempt to make it clear that missions is a fundamental subject of the Bible. We will cover the various points of scripture that talk about this subject and bring it all together.

The Bible is the book of God, revealing His objective, and I intend to reveal that He is all about missions. Missions, therefore, is the essence of the Bible.

CHAPTER ONE

WHAT IS MISSIONS?

I would describe the word "mission" as a purpose upon which a person or a group of people embarks. In Christian parlance, it's a religious work that involves going to a different place to teach about Christianity and/or help others.

For a more definitive description, let us borrow a leaf from the Oxford Advanced Learner's Dictionary:

> an *important* official job that a person or group of people is given to do, especially when they are *sent* to another country... the work of *teaching people about Christianity*, especially in a *foreign* country... particular work which you feel it is your *duty* to do... an important work that is done by a *soldier*; group of soldiers. (emphasis added)[1]

---

[1] A.S. Hornby, ed., *Oxford Advanced Learner's Dictionary, Seventh Edition* (Oxford, UK: Oxford University Press, 2006), 978–979.

The emphasized words and phrases in the Oxford definitions are also present in my opening definition. They are meant to distinguish between Christian missions and more generalized missions. These chief elements must be present to properly convey what Christian missions involve. Any attempt to describe Christian missions must therefore include them.

Below is such a concise attempt:

> Christian missions are all-*important* Christian works whereby people are *sent* out as *duty*-bound officials with a *soldier*-like attitude to *teach* people in *foreign* places about *Christianity*, leading to eternal life in Christ Jesus.

This is my working definition. I have in effect presented the basic facts of missions. Before exploring the Bible to see how this definition plays out, I feel constrained to shed some light on the subject by expatiating each of the emphasized words.

As for the word *all-important,* missions in Christianity occupy a position of utmost significance. For the Christian, missions is to be a cardinal doctrine or way of life. Jesus said in John 5:17, *"My father is working until now, and I*

Myself am working." The Master's instruction for us is simple: *"Do this business… until I come back"* (Luke 19:13). A Spirit-filled Christian cannot be idle and be comfortable. We must just be busily engaged in guided service for the Lord. Finally, Jesus did not depart before giving us our marching orders, that we should go out into the world and spread the gospel (Matthew 28:19–20, Mark 16:15, Luke 24:46–48).

It is equally of paramount importance for the Christian to be *sent*. This was Jesus's final command to us, and He demonstrated and taught it many times during His life on the earth. He sent out the twelve disciples and *"seventy-two others"* (Luke 10:1). Paul the apostle rightly took this seriously and wrote in Romans 10:13–15, *"'Everyone who calls on the name of the Lord will be saved.' …And how are they to hear without a preacher? But how are they to preach unless they are sent?"*

Yes, embarking on missions is a matter of *duty* for Christians. We all have our marching orders from the Master. Having been given a command, we must take upon ourselves the responsibility to spread the message of redemption to all humankind, lest it be lost forever.

As with the *soldier*, the Christian missionary is determined to head for his expedition with a do-or-die attitude, because he sees there is no other option either for himself or those whom he is meant to deliver. The truth is that their lives are at stake.

For Christians, missions is about *"teaching them" everything* (Matthew 28:20). Of course, those who are sent take the time to undertake *teaching* by any means. This often entails living out the life of Christ on the mission field to attract people to Him.

Jesus mostly spoke of going to *foreign* places. Jesus had to pass through Samaria, where He reached men through a woman of low virtue (John 4). Paul's expedition in Acts 13 is referred to as a missionary journey.

But note please that missions aren't always foreign in the sense of going overseas or crossing very great distances. The word can also refer to strange, unfamiliar, or unknown places or cultures. It could also involve different strategies, like picking up jobs in another place. Missions could also take the form of uniquely targeting certain groups or classes of people, professions, or age brackets.

In summary, the target of any form of missions is the people (Revelation 7:10), and it is always done in a bid to introduce or further the knowledge of Christianity, with the ultimate view of helping others attain eternal life in Christ Jesus.

CHAPTER TWO

GOD'S INTENTION SCUTTLED?

Having understood the brilliant style in which the Bible is written, the next task is to locate the real intention of God. We will begin from Genesis.

The first eleven chapters of Genesis are like a prologue to the main story of God's agenda of blessing the whole earth. The history of that blessing then begins with the call of Abraham in Genesis 12.

Genesis 1–3 relates the story of how Adam, through the sin of disobedience, rendered abortive God's earlier plan for man to live forever in His presence in the Garden of Eden. Genesis 4–5 reveal how man continued to procreate and spread himself around the world in accordance with God's will, but they did so in sin.

In Genesis 6, God began to express His displeasure about the sinful state of man. He had to wipe out the whole of creation in Genesis 7. In the process, He salvaged Noah's family.

However, man continued in sin and self-will. This came to a head in Genesis 11, with God scattering man's empire of disobedience. He needed to shop for another man to champion His blessing afresh, and God found that man in Abraham.

The very first thing God did with man after creating him was endow him with blessings:

> So God created man in his own image, in the image of God created he him; male and female created he them. And God blessed them, and God said unto them, *Be fruitful*, and multiply, and replenish the earth, and subdue it: and have dominion over the fish of the sea, and over the fowl of the air, and over *every living thing that moveth upon the earth*. (Genesis 1:27–28, KJV, emphasis added)

This scripture clearly shows that next to the issue of blessing, the intent of God in creating man was for man to bear fruit and spread it across the earth. Which fruit was man expected to bear? Blessedness! This is the main ingredient with which God endowed man. His intention has always been that human beings should spread His blessings to all four corners of the world.

God imparted His person—His wisdom and power to dominate, create, recreate, invent, and renew—into us when He breathed His breath into man's nostrils in Genesis 2:7. He didn't do this to any other creature, not even the very large elephant or man-like gorilla. This is because He expects man, His image, to be creative, like Himself.

Accordingly, even from the beginning, God involved Adam in the process of creation. Adam was blessed with wisdom to partake in the creation work, naming all the animals created by God (Genesis 2:19–20). In fact, God was so confident in Adam's competency that He simply gave credence to whichever names Adam formulated (Genesis 2:19).

In order to bestow blessings on *"every living thing that moveth upon the earth" (Genesis 1:28)*, man has to first dominate his environment, winning it for God and then subduing it. In other words, he must impact it with God's culture.

The failure of man to cover the entire earth and spread God's blessings doesn't go well with God. His pleasure can be seen in Matthew 28:19–20, Mark 16:15, and 2 Corinthians 2:14. We must spread to others the goodness of God that is enveloped in His gospel.

Note that before Adam and Eve bungled their assignment by falling for the deceit of the devil, as Genesis 3:8 tells us, *"they heard the sound of the Lord God walking in the garden in the cool of the day."* This means that it was common for God to come down to interact or associate with them. What a blessed, close, and refreshing relationship they had with the Lord God! This was a delightful fellowship.

Note also that man was supposed to live eternally in God's presence this way. This truth is evident in Genesis 3:22–23: *"'he might stretch out his hand, and take fruit also from the tree of life, and eat, and live forever'—therefore the Lord God sent him out from the Garden of Eden…"* This was the cost of man's first sin.

Man became a *sinner* after this fall (Romans 3:23). Today, we all inherit the sinful nature of our foremost father, Adam, the first sinner. Sin became the nature of man. This means that we are naturally prone to committing sin. And our sinfulness got worse and worse—until it got on the nerves of God:

> Then the Lord saw that the wickedness of mankind was great on the earth, and that every intent of the thoughts of their hearts was only evil continually. So the Lord was sorry that He had made mankind on the earth, and He was grieved in His heart. Then the Lord said, "I will wipe out mankind whom I have created from the

face of the land; mankind, and animals as well, and crawling things, and the birds of the sky. For I am sorry that I have made them." (Genesis 6:5–7)

This informed God's decision to put an end to the whole disturbing situation by wiping out His own creation, for His eyes were too holy to behold iniquity (Habakkuk 1:13).

In Genesis 6, the Lord introduced rainfall which brought about a great flood. For the first time ever, it rained for forty days and forty nights. Graciously, however, in His infinite wisdom, He spared the family of the righteous Noah for purposes of procreation.

God had to reenact the blessing of Genesis 1:28, telling Noah and his sons, *"Be fruitful, and multiply, and replenish the earth"* (Genesis 9:1, KJV). He did this after smelling the sweet savour of the thanksgiving sacrifice given by Noah's family after they emerged from the ark of salvation.

Therefore, everyone in the whole world today is a descendant of Noah, his wife, their three sons—Shem, Ham, and Japheth—and their respective wives.

Man continued to replenish the earth (Genesis 9:19). However, sin and its cousin, self-will, had crept into the nature of man since the fall at Eden, due to the deceit of the serpent. This is because the eyes of Adam and Eve were opened when they discovered that they had a will. Let us read the account from Genesis 3:6–7:

> When the woman saw that the tree was good for food, and that it was a delight to the eyes, and that the tree was desirable to make one wise, she took some of its fruit and ate; and she also gave some to her husband with her, and he ate. *Then the eyes of both of them were opened*, and they knew that they were naked; and they sewed fig leaves together and made themselves waist coverings. (Genesis 3:6–7, emphasis added)

Scripture shows that after eating the forbidden fruit from the tree of the knowledge of good and evil, man began to *see* and *know*. This led to them developing a self-will, which resulted in Adam and Eve adopting outward coverings, clothing made of fig leaves. Consequently, contrary to God's will, rather than spread throughout the world, man instead decided out of self-will to station himself in one spot.

> And they said, "Come, let's build ourselves a city, and a tower whose top will reach into heaven, and let's make a name for ourselves; otherwise we will be scattered abroad over the face of all the earth." (Genesis 11:4)

This was a flagrant departure from the outlook of God in creating man.

Going forward, man developed the unthinkable ambition to build a tower from which he could pry into the very domain of the almighty God. This was an evil desire (Proverbs 21:10).

Note the phrase *"for ourselves"* in the above passage from Genesis 11. Self-will is borne out of pride, and pride in turn produces self-will. The two always go together. Self-actualization is the higher degree of self-will, and the result of these attributes is ultimate destruction. As we read elsewhere in scripture:

> God resists the proud… (James 4:6, NKJV)

> Pride goes before destruction… (Proverbs 16:18, NKJV)

The aim of these people was to resist the will of God by not scattering abroad, and they set out to achieve this by virtue of their oneness.

God had created such a vast earth because He wanted man to spread out and develop it, according to Genesis 1:28. Imagine God the supreme being opening His eyes and seeing His own project scuttled by the disobedience of mere men, nurtured by self-will. Note that self-will is sin. God definitely resisted mankind's move by ensuring that they replenished the earth by spreading His blessings abroad.

God's vision is for man to spread His blessings around the world. This is His delight and aspiration. The Lord had to step down from heaven in Genesis 11, making a grand move to force man to dance to His tune rather than their own. What was His grand move?

> But the Lord came down to see the city and the tower which the sons of men had built. And the Lord said, "Indeed the people are one and they all have one language, and this is what they begin to do; now nothing that they propose to do will be withheld from them. Come, let Us go down

and there confuse their language, that they may not understand one another's speech." *So the Lord scattered them abroad from there over the face of all the earth*, and they ceased building the city. Therefore its name is called Babel… (Genesis 11:5–9, emphasis added)

God had to come down personally because this was His personal project. Tell me, how would man have fulfilled Genesis 1:28 if God had allowed him to stay put at Babel? Instead God did whatever it took to make man obey. He had to summon the supreme heavenly council, just as He had done at creation (Genesis 1:26).

Man is God's blessed creature, the carrier of His blessing—and that blessing has to be used for the purpose of carrying it about and blessing God's entire creation.

For this same reason, the Lord had to organize another scattering in the New Testament (Acts 8) at a time when He had finished revealing and delivering His blessing to those whom He had called out.

God needed another Adam in order to restore man to God's intended outlook (Romans 5:14–15, 1 Corinthians 15:45–47). There had to be a way (John 14:6) through which man could be restored to the blessed state he had been in before the fall.

This brings us to the question of the nature of the blessing of God.

CHAPTER THREE

THE COMING OF THE BLESSING

The blessing of God began with the call of Abraham. As we've established, the first eleven chapters of Genesis is like prologue to God's story. It reveals a generation of people who wouldn't walk with God and commit to His will. The Lord therefore needed to begin again, to raise for Himself a race that would know and follow Him without any recourse to self-will.

He had to seek out the right person, which He found in Abraham.

God knew Abraham's nature, and the man proved through testing that he could be trusted to walk with God. He promptly responded to God's instructions in simple and absolute obedience, often in disregard for the consequences of such obedience. His response to his call (Genesis 12:14) and God's request for the sacrifice of his own child of promise (Genesis 22:1–10) are classic examples of his character and relationship with God. His outlook was that God must be pleased first at all costs, and by whatever means, without the self in the picture or considering the issues of how and why. That is faith!

God's plan required a man who was ready to live by faith and walk with Him. This is what it takes to be able to respond to God's call in Genesis 1:28. This is the kind of man God wanted, the kind He would send out into the world—a man who didn't think of himself and whose main concern was to do the will of God and influence others to do the same.

God had this to say about Abraham: *"For I know him, that he will command his children and his household after him, and they shall keep the way of the Lord…" (Genesis 18:19)*

In light of the above, it goes without saying that Abraham's call fits into our definition of missions. He was the first missionary to ever live. Abraham was sent by God, who Himself left heaven on His own volition on a mission to Eden to salvage mankind from living forever as sinners.

The narrative of the Bible reveals God's agenda, beginning with the call of Abraham in Genesis 12:1–3. Let us examine that call:

> Now the Lord had said unto Abram, Get thee out of thy country, and from thy kindred, and from thy father's house, unto a land that I will shew thee: and I will make of thee a great nation, and I will bless thee,

and make thy name great; and thou shalt be a blessing: and I will bless them that bless thee, and curse him that curseth thee: and *in thee shall all families of the earth be blessed.* (KJV, emphasis added)

The emphasized phrase clearly shows why God called Abraham. That was his assignment. He was sent in order for God's intended blessing to reach the families of the earth, in line with His vision as pronounced in Genesis 1:28.

Abraham clearly answered the call successfully. Even though he had earlier stepped out by following his father as a humble obedient son (Genesis 11:31), he was actually the very called person. This is why Genesis 12:1 begins by saying, *"Now the Lord had said unto Abraham…"* (KJV)

Abraham's father, Terah, had been set to travel to Canaan according to Genesis 11:31. But God had not called him. His decision to come to Canaan had been strictly personal, and therefore *"all things"* were not possible for him because *"with God"* (Matthew 19:26) was missing from His agenda. He died along the way.

God had Canaan in mind as the land from which he would build towards the release of His blessing upon the whole earth, but it would not come through Terah. That man didn't know God. Mission is born out of vision and Terah had no vision. He was only able to go so far as Haran, where he stopped.

I wonder what Terah found there. God had no reason to preserve him, so he died.

In the same way, **your life today must be worthy before God will warrant His continued sustenance.** You won't remain as an encumbrance to God's precious ground (Luke 13:7). Who knows? Maybe God took Terah off the table so he wouldn't constitute an impediment to Abraham.

When Abraham left for Canaan, he did so with two categories of people—family members and converts. He had good following. This shows he was an accomplished evangelist and a successful family man with good leadership qualities, if not also a pastoral calling (Genesis 12:5).

It is also noteworthy that Abraham's obedience was prompt. These are worthy characteristics of the man God would send on missions.

CHAPTER FOUR

ALL THE FAMILIES OF THE EARTH

This phrase in Genesis 12:3 forms the essence of Abraham's call: *"And I will bless those who bless you, and the one who curses you I will curse. And in you all the families of the earth will be blessed."* This last phrase forms the essence of Abraham's call. It is the vision that God sought to fulfill through him. He wanted His blessing to spread throughout the earth.

Why did God pronounce those blessings in Genesis 12:2–3 on Abraham? I would say that it's in view of that conclusive final phrase, which is an offshoot of the pronouncement in Genesis 1:28. The object of God's blessing is *"all the families of the earth."* The Lord has all the earth in view.

It is clear therefore that Abraham and his seed were the people God had in mind to fulfill Genesis 1:28 after the first Adam missed it. The second Adam therefore needed to be Abraham's seed.

Who was that seed of Abraham? The answer is Jesus. This is clear from the genealogy provided in Matthew 1:1–16. Yes, Jesus came forth from Abraham's lineage. Matthew 1:1 pointedly refers to Jesus as the son, or seed, of Abraham.

One might argue that Jesus wasn't the only son of Abraham, that indeed Isaac was the promised son. That is correct. The role of Isaac in the Bible is clear; if he had not been born, we wouldn't have been able to trace the lineage of Jesus to the root of Jesse (Isaiah 11:1, Romans 15:12). If Jesus was to come, Isaac had to open the way.

Note that Abraham had two biological sons, Ishmael, the son of Hagar, and Isaac, the promised son. The promises were spoken to Abraham and to his seed. Scripture does not say "and to seeds," meaning many people, but "and to your seed," meaning one person, who is Christ. (Galatians 3:16, NIV)

This scripture dismisses any doubt as to the truth that Jesus was the seed of Abraham envisaged in Genesis 3:12.[2] It is also very clear that God sent Jesus to the world to save the world.

> For God so loved the world that he gave his one and only Son, that whoever believes in him shall not perish but have eternal life. (John 3:16, NIV)

Jesus therefore was a missionary to the world sent by God. If one asks why Abraham was created, I would

---
[2] See also Galatians 3:14.

answer that it was to pave way for the emergence of Jesus as the blessing of God to the entire world.

Every blessing in the world can be traced back to Jesus. The opposite of all the negative notions mentioned earlier—the fall, curse, spoilage, destruction, deprivation, delusion, hunger, thirst, depression, diseases, and **loss**—are blessings. They can be traced only to Jesus, who declared in John 6:48, *"I am the bread of life"* (NIV). In Him are found all things that pertain to life and godliness (Colossians 1:16–17, 2 Peter 1:3). Only in Him does one find abundant life (John 10:10). He is the way, the truth, and the life (John 14:6). He is the prince of peace (Isaiah 9:6, John 14:27). He has bestowed His riches upon us (1 Corinthians 8:9) and ensured our divine health (Isaiah 53:5).

I dare say that all these indicators of blessing, and many others, are embedded in the package of salvation, which one finds only in Him (Acts 4:12, John 1:3, Matthew 11:28).

Throughout His sojourn on the earth, He busily distributed Himself and the blessing: *"Jesus was going through all the cities and villages, teaching in their synagogues and proclaiming the gospel of the kingdom, and healing every disease and every sickness"* (Matthew 9:35). As if answering the question of why He was here, He declared in Luke 19:10,

"For the Son of Man has come to seek and to save that which was lost."

That is a missionary speaking. This was the outlook of Jesus, His mission statement and primary business.

Do you have a reason for living? Luke 19:10 provides the terms of reference for the missionary. The same calling is true for every Christian.

GLIMPSES OF THE BLESSING

Let's consider ways in which the Bible reveals Jesus Christ as the personification of God's blessing to the world.

He was a provider. At Cana of Galilee, as recorded in John 2, Jesus miraculously provided even sweeter wine at the marriage of His hosts. He makes life sweeter. He adds to life. He leaves His hosts better than He meets them. He is keenly interested in holy wedlock and would do anything to support it.

As a provider, He didn't only feed His hearers spiritually but never let them go unsatisfied physically. He demonstrated this in John 6 when he fed more than four thousand people with five loaves of bread and two fish.

In Matthew 15, He fed more than five thousand with seven loaves and a few fish.

He turns little into much. He overwhelms His beneficiaries with His providence, just as He did to Peter in Luke 5.

He was a helper. He came to the aid of a man who had no one to help him (John 5:2–9). This hopeless man had been trapped in the same hopelessly miserable situation for thirty-eight years. Jesus singled him out and gave him a new lease of life.

He healed those with leprosy. People with leprosy were ostracized as outcasts in those days. Not only did Jesus welcome them, but He also touched and healed them, restoring them to their earlier state of life. He restores. He refines and perfects whoever comes to Him. This was a rare show of love and compassion (Mark 1:40–42, Luke 17:12–19).

He rescued a harlot. He came to the rescue of a woman who had been caught squarely in the act of contravening a very popular law against immorality (John 8:3–11). This woman was minutes away from a cruel death by stoning, having been judged as deserving death under the obnoxious law. Jesus saved her by applying the wonderfully rare art of wisdom.

He succoured a widow. He also came to the aid of a *widow* who was being escorted to a cemetery to bury her *only son. In Luke 7:13,* Jesus spoke to her compassionately, telling her, *"Do not go on weeping."* He then touched the coffin and raised the young man: *"And the dead man sat* *up and began to speak"* (John 7:15). Thus, He prevented a widow from being childless.

He reached out to a lost city. He saved a whole city in John 4. He had to pass through Samaria even though it was unbecoming for Jews to do so in those days. It was seen as a debasement to associate with their women at all, but Jesus had an open conversation with a known Samarian prostitute in order to quench His thirst for seeing people get saved. He humbled Himself because He had to spread blessings and bear fruit.

A salient lesson here is that Jesus demonstrated to His disciples the necessity of seeking and saving that which is lost. In doing so, he lived out the message of Mathew 6:33: *"But seek first His kingdom and His righteousness, and all these things will be provided to you."*

By exploiting an opportunity to save a soul, he was able to save a whole city. This is a missionary exploit.

Another lesson is that a disciple should be ready to witness for Christ in any given situation.

He healed the blind. On another occasion, Jesus demonstrated that He was God by creating a brand-new pair of eyes for a man who was born blind (John 9:1–7). The Bible says that He *"spat on the ground, and made mud from the saliva, and applied the mud to his eyes" (John 9:6).* He created man with mud in the beginning. For this blind man, He only had to complete His creation using the same method.

He saved a criminal at the last minute. A final example of good works I must not fail to call attention to is the truth that Jesus demonstrated His power to admit entrants into heaven (Luke 23:39–43). Hear Him save a condemned but repentant sinner at the last minute in Luke 23:43: *"Truly I say to you, today you will be with Me in Paradise."*

This goes to show that He has power not just to save the lost, but also to grant eternal life. The kingdom of heaven is His.

During His time on the earth, He was always ready to do good, even when it wasn't convenient, even at the point of death. He seized every opportunity to win souls. He healed, delivered, restored, salvaged, and saved all those He came across.

How can one bring up all the good works the Lord did during His time in the world in just one book? According to John 21:25, *"But there are also many other things which Jesus did, which, if they were written in detail, I expect that even the world itself would not contain the books that would be written."*

I have therefore mentioned these few examples of the blessings of God which Jesus spread about. They are profound examples. God gave Jesus as a blessing to the world, according to John 3:16. He is a gift. His coming has been in accordance with God's program as written in scripture (Isaiah 7:14, Micah 5:2, Isaiah 53). The whole of the Bible is indeed all about Jesus! He is the central theme.

CHAPTER FIVE

A CHRISTIAN, AN EVANGELIST

The Greek word *evangel* simply connotes good news, or good tidings (Luke 2:10–11). Good news refers to a message of redemption or salvation, such as a proclamation of the coming of a Saviour. Carrying or proclaiming good news is *evangelism*, while the carrier or proclaimer of that good news is an evangelist. This is all about soul-winning. So an evangelist is a soul-winner.

Jesus spent all His time distributing the blessings of His Father, bearing fruit in fulfillment of God's outlook in Genesis 1:28. So faithful and committed was He that He didn't leave any stone unturned in living out that vision. He continued to teach wherever He went and instructed His followers to do the same.

Indeed, as far as He was concerned, a follower was a soul-winner. Hear Him:

> Follow me, and I will make you fishers of men. (Matthew 4:19)

> Follow me, and I will make you become
> fishers of men. (Mark 1:17)

Jesus made these statements to people He was meeting for the first time. This demonstrates that the calling to win souls is intended for every follower of Jesus, regardless of how young or old they are in their faith. In other words, a newly born-again Christian even today is meant to be a soul-winner.

When Jesus called people in the Bible, He did so with a view toward making them fishers of men. This was His aim. Today, you are to become a person who is determined to fish, to seek others from the waters in order to save them. This was Jesus's declaration in Luke 19:10.

I don't know how best to share blessings and bear fruit other than to minister salvation through which *"all these things"* (Matthew 6:33) could be added to men.

However, the act of making someone a fisher of men happens through followership.

Evangelism invariably matures from witnessing to others within one's vicinity to a larger scale by being sent out to the mission field. In mentoring His followers, the Lord began with one-on-one witnessing, as in the cases of Nicodemus (John 3), the woman of Sychar in Samaria (John 4), and Zacchaeus (Luke 19:1–9). He went with them to various places to preach (Luke 4:43), including open-air crusades like the Sermon on the Mount (Matthew 5–7).

In short, His mainstay was to encourage evangelism through different strategies to different targets.

Everywhere Jesus went, He dwelled with them. He seized every opportunity to teach and show them how to be a blessing. Not only did He engage in preaching, teaching, healing, working of diverse miracles, and raising the dead, but He also exploited several training strategies in making them fishers of men, including missionary field trips.

But He didn't do this without first empowering them:

> And he called the twelve together and gave them power and authority over all demons and to cure diseases, and he sent them out to proclaim the kingdom of God and to heal. (Luke 9:1–2)

Later, He sent seventy others:

> After this the Lord appointed seventy-two others and sent them on ahead of him, two by two, into every town and place where he himself was about to go. (Luke 10:1)

He took them on periodic retreats (Mark 6:31). And to teach humility, servanthood, and love, He washed their feet (John 13:4–9). This had the spiritual significance of preparing their feet—their means of moving—to be beautiful, honourable, and fruitful in publishing the gospel of peace and bringing glad tidings of good things (Romans 10:15, Isaiah 52:7).

In light of this, I see Jesus as a successful leader and apostle. He was able to effectively disciple and equip His followers. He didn't go to all this trouble just for the fun of it; He knew that He needed to empty Himself into them in view of His vision. His works included preaching, performing diverse signs and wonders, praying, feeding the multitudes, making visitations, counselling, soul-winning, and going on missions.

This begs a few questions. Why did He perform all these great works? What was His main goal or vision? The answer is evangelism.

He died after doing all those works, finishing it on the cross. The moment He rose from the dead and had a final opportunity to address His followers, He focused on His main mission: evangelism, the act of going out into the world to win souls. He commissioned His followers only after having paid the supreme price. This was when the occasion was ripe, when He had a final opportunity to declare why He went about doing good.

Who can say that the other works aren't important? They are. They're important because they serve the ancillary or supportive purpose of soul-winning. They serve to lay the groundwork or make soul-winning attractive. The crucial aim of the Master is getting people saved.

At this point, I must press home the glaring biblical truth that any Christian gathering that doesn't focus on the salvation of souls is a colossal failure, like a football game that produces no goals. May we not play to a draw with the kingdom of the devil! May we never fail to gladden the heart of God with our programs.

As the Master said, *"I tell you that in the same way, there will be more joy in heaven over one sinner who repents than over ninety-nine righteous people who have no need of repentance"* (Luke 15:7).

First, this shows that God's heart wouldn't be gladdened over any Christian endeavour that doesn't result in soul-winning, even if there are many other works, including powerful worship, signs, and wonders.

Second, note that the Bible emphasizes the importance of a believer's *repentance,* not just their membership in a church. Only the repented soul makes heaven!

Third, and very importantly, this scripture underscores the truth that of all the acts of a Christian, the one that represents God's heart cry most is soul-winning. This is what the Lord God sent His only begotten Son to die for.

This is why I believe that Christians who don't serve to satisfy God's heartbeat cannot be said to be profiting Him. It's also why the Lord Jesus had to come from heaven to be a blessing to the world.

Having trained and ordained His disciples, Jesus was able to confidently and responsibly give them the mandate described as the Great Commission. *Go Ye…*

CHAPTER SIX

"GO YE…"

"And he said unto them, Go ye into all the world, and preach the gospel to every creature. He that believeth and is baptized shall be saved; but he that believeth not shall be damned" (Mark 16:15–16, KJV).

The same command is recorded by the apostle Matthew in a broader and more detailed manner:

> All power is given unto me in heaven and in earth. Go ye therefore, and teach all nations, baptizing them in the name of the Father, and of the Son, and of the Holy Ghost: teaching them to observe all things whatsoever I have commanded you: and, lo, I am with you always, even unto the end of the world. (Matthew 28:18–20, KJV)

In this way, He scattered His followers all over the world, for them to in turn scatter His blessings and bear the fruit of the gospel.

The question now is simple: to whom is that command directed, and who is expected to obey it by carrying on the work of distributing the blessings of God, seeking and saving those who are lost?

The answer is equally simple: His disciples.

Jesus's disciples were the group of followers who were found together at the place where the Lord appeared to them after rising from the dead. These were the saved ones who had followed well enough to internalize their Master's crucial vision.

But how do we define a disciple today? He is *"a person who believes in and helps to spread another's teaching, a follower... one of the twelve apostles of Christ."*[3]

Clearly, we cannot be said to be part of the very first twelve, but the fact stands that we are believers and followers today. Paul was also a follower, even though he never followed Jesus when He was alive. However, he followed after the Lord's death and resurrection and was able to serve the master more than all the rest (1 Corinthians 15:10). He followed more assiduously once the

---

[3] *Webster's Universal Dictionary and Thesaurus* (New Lanark, UK: Gaddes & Grosset,, 2003), 154.

scales fell off his eyes (Acts 9:18). When the scales of worldliness, deception, religion, shadow-chasing, and sleepiness fall off one's eyes, such a Christian is on his way to becoming a disciple.

A person is also qualified to be a disciple if he is a believer who helps spread the teachings of Jesus. I therefore am of the opinion that a disciple is any believer who is disciplined enough to be willing and ready to spread the gospel.

In view of Luke 9:62, Matthew 11:29, Hosea 6:3, and Luke 9:23, we must all be disciples.

If we are followers of the Lord Jesus Christ, the Great Commission has been directed at us. Jesus had us in mind when He made that command. We have the responsibility to go into the whole world and preach the gospel to every creature.

If you have become a believer, thank God. However, if you haven't been disciplined enough to follow the Lord and also help spread His teachings, you have the obligation to positively respond to it now as a high and holy calling.

In short, evangelism is for every believer. If you don't conform to this ideal, I'm sorry to say that you are not pleasing your saviour. We should not be disappointing believers. The text of Mark 16:15 is like a dying declaration by Jesus, which He gave us during His final address to His in-person followers. That command came out from a deeply constrained heart.

As pointed out earlier in this book, the Master worked, led, preached, taught, and finally bled and died to show the way. He paid the supreme price! Afterward the all-important work needed to continue in order for His mission to be fulfilled. That's why He entrusted it to you and me, His followers.

How will He feel if He finds us sitting at ease in Zion, not obeying the Great Commission? I believe we will be breaking the heart of the Lord. We must not be disappointing believers. You must give everything it takes to see His mission fulfilled. You must carry the blessing!

I hope you realize that if you are already found in Him, you already carry that blessing. When you know this, you can't afford to carry it for nothing. You must operate that blessing and advance it.

Jesus must be known and carried to the whole earth, beginning from our immediate milieu. This is the essence of Acts 1:8: *"but you will receive power when the Holy Spirit has come upon you; and you shall be My witnesses both in Jerusalem and in all Judea, and Samaria, and as far as the remotest part of the earth."*

The Lord didn't send the Holy Spirit to believers just for us to speak in tongues and see visions. This is not to say that speaking in tongues and seeing visions aren't essential to the purpose of the Holy Spirit, but that purpose is first and foremost focused on empowering us to reach the entire world for Him with His blessing. We must participate. This is why the earlier disciples did everything they did in going out and preaching the gospel.

Mark 16:20 says, *"And they went out and preached everywhere, while the Lord worked with them, and confirmed the word with the signs that followed."* This is the minimum expectation of any believer: to go forth in obedience.

After believers go forth, signs will follow. This kind of success is accomplished because they obey the commandment to *"tarry"* first (Luke 24:29). This was the result of the Pentecostal event recorded in Acts 2. Tarrying is the secret behind the apostle Paul's success (Galatians 1:15–18); it is a strategy he learned from his Master Jesus (Luke 4:1–14, Acts 10:38).

These writings in the Bible serve to fashion, serve as groundwork, enable, complete, and perfect the vision of God regarding missions.

CHAPTER SEVEN

DISCIPLES SCATTERED

According to Luke 24:49, the disciples were to remain in Jerusalem only until they were endowed with power: *"And behold, I am sending the promise of My Father upon you; but you are to stay in the city <u>until</u> you are clothed with power from on high"* (emphasis added).

Thereafter, they were to scatter—and their failure to scatter led to what is recorded in Acts 8:4.

First, let's recall the story of the tower of Babel in the Old Testament (Genesis 11:1–4). This same scenario repeated itself in the New Testament. We see it play out in the lives of the disciples after Jesus's departure.

Despite Jesus's excellent leadership and marching orders, the first disciples to see Him in the flesh decided to misbehave like the men of old. By way of omission, they too disobeyed the will of God in deciding to remain in one place, Jerusalem, instead of carrying His blessing to all the world.

The Lord's instructions were for them to tarry in Jerusalem only until they were empowered by the Holy Spirit. Accordingly, they *"returned to Jerusalem with great joy, and were continually in the temple praising God"* (Lk 24:52–53) Good! They obediently remained in the upper room until they were truly endowed with power from on high on the day of Pentecost.

One would think they would immediately head out to spread the good news. But no, they did not.

Granted, they were to begin witnessing in Jerusalem (Acts 1:8). However, they lost cognizance of the determinant word, *until* (Luke 24:49). They witnessed quite well in Jerusalem until the need arose for some reorganization among the church as it expanded. This resulted in the appointment or ordination of deacons in Acts 6.

Was this not an indication that Jerusalem had been saturated with the gospel? The disciples' next move, logically, should have been for them to scatter according to the will and direction of God, with Jerusalem serving as the mission base.

However, they failed to see it that way. Jerusalem was their comfort zone!

Do the saints in our proverbial Jerusalems need no more ministerial attention? Of course they do. They need to continually grow in grace by way of teaching, exhortation, and encouragement. This is the essence of pastoral ministry. But brethren who have grown and are mature enough to raise others should be **sent** out to other places to seek, raise, and establish new Christians in faith, especially where the people are yet unreached.

As I've already pointed out, other aspects of ministry are also important. However, as the Lord took time to emphasize, the ministry of bringing in the lost is the most crucial. This is the heartbeat of God, especially in these latter days. The Lord said, *"Go out… and press upon them to come in, so that my house will be filled"* (Luke 14:23).

Even the apostle Peter failed to understand the heavenly signal in Acts 10 when God declared to him in a trance that he should have a heart also for the Gentiles. Unfortunately, this calling to minister to the Gentiles was withdrawn from Peter without him quenching his supposed hunger for unreached souls (Acts 10:16).

Paul was the ready instrument at that time (Acts 9). It looks like Peter would have reached many more Gentiles if he had been obedient. Being the leader of the disciples, God might have intended him to spearhead the outreach to the Gentiles.

Be that as it may, the disciples clearly weren't meant to tarry forever in Jerusalem, but rather to scatter as soon as it was practical after being endowed with power from on high. They failed to move out voluntarily until persecution arose from opposing religionists, with the tacit support of government agencies. This forced them to disperse abroad.

The scattering began with the stoning of Stephen, a deacon turned evangelist, in Acts 7 and came to a head with the government-authorized molestation of believers by Saul, who *"made havock of the church, entering into every house, and haling men and women committed them to prison. Therefore they that were scattered abroad went everywhere preaching the word"* (Acts 8:3–4, KJV).

Praise the Lord! The end of this persecution made it a good problem for the disciples to have. These hitherto Jerusalem-stationed followers of Jesus found themselves scattered everywhere indeed, preaching the word. This was the will of God, forced to come to pass involuntarily.

Clearly, God was aware of this persecution. He allowed it. It may not be wrong to say, as many claim, that God Himself organized it! He was simply waiting to corner Paul, the chief persecutor, and saddle him with his own mission to the uttermost parts of the earth.

It is plausible to conclude that God came down from heaven to organize this saga. Recall that He had organized a scattering of this nature before, at the tower of Babel. God will do whatever it takes for the gospel to be preached everywhere, for the lost to be saved, especially where the gospel has never before been heard. Jesus, the blessed Messiah, must be made known everywhere!

CHAPTER EIGHT

PERPETRATING THE BLESSING

The aim of this chapter is to show the necessity of going into missions and sending others in the fulfillment of our Lord and Saviour's yearning in the Great Commission.

> …for "Everyone who calls on the name of the Lord will be saved."
>
> How then are they to call on Him in whom they have not believed? How are they to believe in Him whom they have not heard? And how are they to hear without a preacher? But how are they to preach unless they are sent? Just as it is written: "How beautiful are the feet of those who bring good news of good things!" (Romans 10:13–15)

The most salient message flowing from this important passage is this: *"Everyone who calls on the name of the Lord will be saved."* This scripture presupposes that a certain number of people are lost and in need of salvation. This is the problem at hand.

We may go further to reason that the lost shall be saved if they call upon the name of the Lord. A sad truth, however, is that many people don't even know they are lost, while many who know that they're lost do not know what to do or how to get saved.

This situation is rightly captured in Joel 3:14: *"Multitudes, multitudes in the valley of decision! For the day of the Lord is near in the valley of decision."*

This is why the apostle Paul, the greatest missionary ever, came up with this golden composition in Romans 10. As the learned person he was, he began with a deductive logical argument, identifying the problem and closing the passage by stating the reward awaiting obedient disciples who help bring about the solution.

Paul first makes us see that calling on the name of the Lord is the panacea for salvation. He then goes on to brilliantly rationalize the necessity of believing in the saviour in order to be saved, to hear in order to believe, to preach in order to be heard, and to send in order for the preacher to go.

To my mind, this is a strong persuasive argument. Paul was a lawyer indeed, capable of convincing and moving anyone, especially the believer, to carry his cross and comply with this call to service in line with Mark 16:15 and Genesis 1:28.

There is no doubt that *"all have sinned and fall short of the glory of God"* (Romans 3:23). This is why we are being called to respond to His clarion call. The truth is that the enemy is busy doing his best to attract those who are still in the valley of decision. He leaves no stone unturned to persuade, seduce, deceive, lure, entice, and coerce them to his side so they go with him into eternal damnation. This is why the heartbeat of God is that the lost must be saved.

Another crucial truth is that time is fast running out on us. And sadly, it's running out for those who are yet to be reached with the gospel. We're talking about not only those around us but too many others in the outermost parts of the world. Many places are still closed to the gospel due to distance, unfavourable terrain, ignorance, backwardness, or anti-gospel legislation.

If all have sinned and come short of the glory of the Lord, thank God for the provision for restoration in Romans 6:23, which says, *"For the wages of sin is death, but the gracious gift of God is eternal life in Christ Jesus our Lord."* This is good news.

The crucial challenge, however, is to get the lost to call on the name of Jesus to be saved: *"And there is salvation in no one else; for there is no other name under heaven that has been given among mankind by which we must be saved"* (Acts 4:12). The Saviour Himself declared in John 14:6, *"I am the way, and the truth, and the life; no one comes to the Father except through Me."*

This goes to show that unless we earnestly take heed of the Great Commission, we're wasting our precious time. We need to be reaching out to save the hopelessly lost with the name of the Lord. If not, we sadden the heart of our Master. We must give up whatever might be hindering us and earnestly answer the call of the Great Commission.

As disciples, we are to set to work in the following areas of service: going, sending, giving, or praying. Since the Great Commission is a call to all believers, we are to be involved in all of these areas. Each is necessary and should form the outlook of every true Christian.

However, as it's practically impossible to serve in all these ways, we may only fully delve into one or two of them, even while we practice all four in our day-to-day lives.

There is a fifth area of service, though, that is equally germane to the fulfillment of the Great Commission, and therefore we must discuss it: the role for m**issions mobilizers**. These missionaries go about canvassing to raise awareness of missions, using all sorts of strategies to prepare people for the necessity of participating in Christian missions.

Chapter Eight: Perpetrating the Blessing

The necessity for mobilization cannot be overemphasized. Even though many Christian leaders claim to understand the importance of missions, especially in these latter days, a vast many believers know next to nothing about them. I wonder why.

Furthermore, where there is awareness of missions, little or nothing is being done to energize church members to get involved. This is why mission mobilizers must exploit every strategy at their disposal to create awareness and encourage Christians to enrol in the task.

The book in your hand, for example, is a mobilizing tool. In effect, you are being urged to enter into the mission and play your part in it.

Apart from this, there are people who specialize in training aspiring missionaries. They are referred to as **missionary trainers**. Note that they too must have undergone training for missions, just as mobilizers have and indeed all other Christians who seek to play a role. Training is simply necessary for anyone who intends to succeed in his missionary calling.

Furthermore, every missionary, regardless of speciality, goes to the field from time to time. This affords them a first-hand feel of the realities on the field and goes a long way in encouraging missionaries who serve in the same field.

However, those who depart from their own locality—like Abraham, Jesus, and Paul—and travel to another place to propagate the gospel are known as field missionaries. They cannot practice their missions work alone. They must have stepped out from a group of like-minded disciples.

> Now there were prophets and teachers at Antioch, in the church that was there: Barnabas, Simeon who was called Niger, Lucius of Cyrene, Manaen who had been brought up with Herod the tetrarch, and Saul. While they were serving the Lord and fasting, the Holy Spirit said, "Set Barnabas and Saul apart for Me for the work to which I have called them." Then, when they had fasted, prayed, and laid their hands on them, they sent them away.
>
> So, being sent out by the Holy Spirit, they went… (Acts 13:1–4)

Everyone in the group must equally go, either in terms of sending, praying together, or supporting field missionaries by giving out of their resources. Everyone is jointly involved in all the areas of service.

Chapter Eight: Perpetrating the Blessing

If for any reason a Christian cannot go on missions, he should be actively involved in at least one other area. They are all equally important endeavours so long as the effort is geared towards the furtherance of seeking and saving the lost.

The point is that you are to sincerely discover your own lot and delve into it while working in concert with others. Many of the disciples of Jesus, if not all of them, ended up missionaries. They actively participated in almost all these areas of service. Nevertheless, one man excelled in all areas. Paul was an apostle of Jesus, even though he had learned of Him only in the Spirit.

Today, you and I ought to be able to serve the Lord like Paul did. In the next chapter, we shall examine his life as a model missionary, focusing on his first missionary journey as recorded in Acts 13–15.

CHAPTER NINE

PAUL THE MISSIONARY

Paul received his calling on the very first day of His salvation, the day he met the Lord Jesus. I am of the view that anyone who really encounters the Lord Jesus will immediately perceive a deep-seated calling in their heart to some area of service. The vision may be faint and indefinite, or it may assume a miniature dimension at first, but it grows larger and more defined over time as long as it isn't abandoned or disregarded.

In the case of Paul, it was clear from the beginning that he was going to be sent. Consider his conversation with the Lord Jesus. He didn't need to be told that the power accosting him was from the Lord. This informed his reaction in Acts 9:6: *"Lord, what wilt thou have me to do?"* That question naturally comes to the mind for anyone who encounters the Lord; the call to service is usually the mindset of the Lord.

Paul immediately swung into action. When he realized the magnitude and gravity of his assignment (Acts 9:15), he departed into the "wilderness" (Galatians 1:15–19) before his revelation, just as it happened with Jesus

(Matthew 4:1–2, Luke 4:1–2). He then joined the church in Jerusalem for ministerial services until he was commissioned into the ministry in Acts 13:1–3.

Upon receiving their call, a minister is usually commissioned by way of the laying on of hands and anointing with oil, and this usually occurs in the presence of a praying local assembly. This is the sending point.

The laying on of hands indicates the impartation of ministerial gifts necessary for the call (Acts 6:6, 1 Timothy 4:14). Anointing a person with oil indicates a separation or marking out of the called into the calling; this is a symbol of the presence of the Holy Spirit. However, I am of the opinion that what really empowers the anointed person is the prayer and laying on of hands. It's interesting to note that even though anointing with oil was the main approach taken in the Old Testament (Exodus 39:7, 1 Samuel 16:13), it is rather meant mainly for healing the sick in the New Testament (Mark 6:13, James 5:14).

Note also that commissioning is usually preceded by a minister's personal preparation and training. Jesus and Paul underwent personal preparation, and Jesus remains our ultimate model. He kept on learning from God the Father (John 5:30, 8:26–28). Part of his training involved learning to be obedient in suffering (Hebrews 5:8).

Chapter Nine: Paul the Missionary

As with Abraham, Paul obeyed God immediately on his first missionary journey. He worked in the company of his co-labourer Barnabas and personal assistant John Mark. He was led by the Holy Spirit on an evangelistic expedition that took him through Gentile cities like Seleucia, Cyprus, Salamis, Paphos, Perga, Antioch, Iconium, Lystra, and Derbe.

It was the custom of these missionaries to enter synagogues and other places, public or private, as led by the Holy Spirit for the purpose of preaching the gospel and winning converts for the Lord.

Their first extraordinary encounter took place at Paphos (Acts 13:6–12). The deputy leader of that city, Sergius Paulus, had invited them because he desired to hear the word of God. Coincidentally, when Paul and Barnabas arrived, Sergius Paulus had with him a Jewish sorcerer and false prophet by the name of Barjesus.

As Paul preached the gospel of the Lord Jesus Christ, Barjesus opposed it. But Paul wouldn't allow any agent of the devil to come between him and winning souls. Moved by the Holy Spirit, Paul made the following pronouncement again Barjesus:

> You who are full of all deceit and fraud,
> you son of the devil, you enemy of all

> righteousness, will you not stop making crooked the straight ways of the Lord? Now, behold, the hand of the Lord is upon you, and you will be blind and not see the sun for a time. (Acts 13:10–11)

I believe this is what it means to feel "holy" anger. The result?

> And immediately a mist and a darkness fell upon him, and he went about seeking those who would lead him by the hand. Then the proconsul believed when he saw what had happened, being amazed at the teaching of the Lord. (Acts 13:11–12)

This goes to show that signs and wonders follow Christians who engage in service, especially when it comes to soul-winning. We see this in the lives of Paul and several other disciples who were on the move.

It also shows that missionaries will encounter opposition, as the devil is always out to oppose the free flow of *"the gospel, for it is the power of God for salvation to everyone who believes…"* (Romans 1:16). This is part of the reason that the Master gave power to His disciples in Luke 19:10.

Can you see the effect? The wonder shown to Sergius Paulus in Paphos convinced him to believe the gospel of Christ and he got saved. As John 4:48 tells us, *"Unless you people see signs and wonders, you simply will not believe"* (John 4:48).

The effect of signs and wonders during soul-winning is enormous. Preaching with expertise and having a good command of English would normally have a persuasive effect on any audience. But when the audience experiences signs and wonders, with or without this expertise, there are always results. Signs and wonders invariably show forth when there have been ample prayers.

Ask any successful missionary and they'll confess to you that signs and wonders are key. This is why they don't have to beg people to listen.

At Antioch in Pisidia, Paul seized the opportunity of his invitation to exhort the people to teach the gospel of salvation by challenging and calling his audience into believing in the prophecy and fulfillment of the death and resurrection of Jesus (Acts 13:14–52).

The expectation of the Lord is for His followers to seize every available opportunity to present Him and offer one's audience salvation. Jesus did just that in John 4.

However, after a successful gospel outreach, the Jews in the region orchestrated a huge persecution against Paul and Barnabas out of envy, which got them expelled from the region. This is typical of a really biting presentation of true gospel. It's bound to attract persecution, usually out of envy, even by fellow believers.

Another salient detail of this particular outreach is that in-depth knowledge of the scriptures is of the utmost importance to any missionary. Paul began by recapping the days of the Israelites in Egypt, quoting the prophets copiously and zeroing in on one's justification by faith. This is similar to the style of the apostle Peter in Acts 2, the deacon Stephen in Acts 7, and others too.

This example of Paul's demonstration of a wide spectrum of knowledge in expounding scripture reveals the importance of sending highly educated people in missions.

Also noteworthy is the truth that were it not for Paul's personality, he would not have been able to carry the gospel before highly placed men like King Agrippa and Governor Festus (Acts 25–26). Apart from this, he was always the main speaker (Acts 14:12) while Barnabas stood by for moral support and to intercede while Paul spoke. They had a powerful spiritual collaboration.

I find it meaningful to point out that Barnabas was mainly a pastor and teacher (Acts 11:22–26), not an evangelist *per se*. This is partly why Paul did all the talking (Acts 14:12). This goes to show that evangelists aren't the only ones to embark on missions. The ministry of the teacher has proved very necessary for an evangelist's success. Paul and Barnabas were both missionaries, in fulfillment of the teaching aspect of the Great Commission.

Paul had another extraordinary encounter at Lystra (Acts 14:8–22). In the company of Barnabas, he healed a certain congenitally disabled man. This miracle made the people mistake the duo for two of their own gods, almost offering sacrifices to them. Paul and Barnabas resisted the move and seized the opportunity to point the people to God.

Despite this, they stoned Paul and dragged him out of the city, leaving him for dead. Why on earth? Certain unbelieving Jews from Antioch and Iconium had traced these two missionaries there and poisoned the minds of the people against them.

I was shocked to read in Acts 14:21 that Paul returned a few days thereafter to continue exhorting and encouraging the people to abide in the faith. What a soldier! Elsewhere he wrote that he would be done for if he ever failed to preach the gospel (1 Corinthians 9:16).

This is a true missionary, diehard disciple, and avowed soul-winner.

At Iconium, following Paul's declaration of the gospel in the synagogue, which yielded many souls among Jews and Gentiles alike, the unbelieving Jews stirred up the Gentiles against them, poisoning their minds against the gospel (Acts 14:1–6). This led the duo to stay back for a long time, testifying of the efficacy of the word in order to convince them. The Lord honoured His word by providing signs and wonders (Mark 16:17–20).

The persecution continued despite this, and Paul and Barnabas had to flee again. This was in accordance with the Lord's instruction in Luke 9:5 and 10:10.

Derbe was the last city they touched with the gospel of salvation on their first missionary journey. They retraced their way back to Antioch, their commissioning church and mission base.

It is noteworthy that on their way back they stopped at each of the cities they had reached with the gospel and took time to ascertain the salvation of their converts, encouraging them to remain steadfast in the faith.

Following up with new converts is germane to the success of winning souls. The soul-winner has a duty to make sure his fruits abide in order to fulfill the Master's expectation as laid down in John 15:16: *"I have chosen you, and ordained you, that ye should go and bring forth fruit, and that your fruit should remain…"* (KJV)

The Lord's emphasis here is that our fruits should remain and continue to take hold. What would be the essence of obeying Him by going out and bearing fruit if the fruit of the endeavour didn't have a lasting effect? This is why the soul-winner is enjoined to make the effort to go back and look on his converts and be sure they are abiding in the faith.

For a convert, seeing one's soul-winner again—and again, if need be—is weighty to their conviction. This type of follow-up should be done at the earliest opportunity in order to prevent the danger of the seed falling on stony ground (Matthew 13:5–6, 19–21). Furthermore, to prevent the danger of the seed falling among thorns (Matthew 13:7, 22), it is noteworthy that Paul didn't leave his converts without appointing leaders to look after them (Matthew 14:23).

Paul achieved much by tarrying on his knees until Christ could be formed in them (Galatians 4:19). This is the most crucial duty of the evangelist. Both legwork and kneework must go together for anyone to succeed. This is especially important for the evangelist, as he is in a direct tug of war against the god of this world for unsaved souls.

At the end of this first missionary journey, Paul and Barnabas returned to Antioch to give a full report of the grace of God upon them for the work that they had fulfilled (Acts 14:26).

Think about that! It was work indeed, and it was fulfilling. They were fulfilled because they had accomplished the Lord's bidding, the heartbeat of God for all Christians.

I believe that all the leaders and members of a sending church must also be fulfilled, because they paid their own price, interceding for the sent preacher and the souls to be won, and then watching over the newly won young Christians.

When they return to their home base, missionaries abide with their brethren to refresh themselves and go back out to save more souls. This is the advisable practice of all Christian missionaries. Their duty is not to remain too long in any given church after planting it. As rightly demonstrated by Paul, the new church ought to be left in the care of pastors and teachers whose ministry it is to nurture them into maturity, so they too can go out and found more churches.

Of course, in deserving cases the missionary may remain in one place for the purpose of raising and training indigenous believers before sending them out. Very importantly, serving Christians must periodically take time apart from their mission to refresh (Mark 6:31). Missionaries have a duty to demonstrate the life of Christ wherever they are, in order to disciple growing believers and attract others to the faith.

Chapter Nine: Paul the Missionary

Time and space don't permit me to fully relay all the exploits of Paul, either alone or in league with other missionaries. These exploits can be found from Acts 13–28. It will be sufficient to mention just a few of his other experiences. He was led by the Holy Spirit (Acts 16:9, 18:9–11), mysteriously rescued by God (Acts 16:25–26), raised the dead (Acts 20:7–12), declared himself ready to die for the name of the Lord Jesus Christ (Acts 21:10–14), rode in the king's carriage guarded by two hundred soldiers (Acts 23:23–31), heard God (Acts 27:23–24), and miraculously survived a venomous snake bite (Acts 28:3–6). To the glory of God, Paul accomplished his calling (2 Timothy 2:7).

CHAPTER TEN

GOD'S PROVIDENCE

Throughout all the engagements in the book of the Acts, the issue of feeding, lodging, and clothing the apostles never comes up. God never allowed this to be a concern. His servants weren't bothered about these considerations because they were preoccupied with seeking and saving the lost. The Lord knew He was going to *"supply all [their] need according to his riches in glory by Christ Jesus"* (Philippians 4:19, KJV) and *"make all grace overflow to [them], so that, always having all sufficiency in everything, [they] may have an abundance for every good deed"* (2 Corinthians 9:8).

I know of a missionary who could afford to give me a whooping fifteen thousand naira as a wedding present in 1995. That was a huge amount of money in those days, especially coming from a serving missionary. Little did he know that he bought me my first matrimonial bed! I remember that he also engaged my services as a legal practitioner for the purchase of a vast landed property.

Missionaries ordinarily do not lack! They are always powered by God.

Note that the word *need* in Philippians 4:19 (KJV) is singular. We only have one need. Our only need as a follower of Christ is to look up to Him, *"the author and perfecter of our faith"* (Hebrews 12:2).

That was exactly how it happened for the disciples. They never lacked anything good! This is the real tenet of Matthew 6:33. Because missionaries seek first the kingdom of God and His righteousness, they normally don't lack any good thing, according to Psalm 34:10.

How could a person leave everything behind to follow God and then lack anything good? If a missionary doesn't leave everything behind, of course, they could lack; they may also lack if they labour under a spirit of fear or faithlessness, serve the god of their belly, look up to other men, or are otherwise uncommitted to the Master.

Understand that prosperity isn't merely about the acquisition of money and other forms of physical riches. It's about the mastery of wealth! When you don't worship money, it pursues you, allowing you to distribute it to others as a blessing, especially in the service of the Lord, who is the owner of all wealth. When you are content, you are prosperous!

God makes adequate provision for missions, missionaries, and missionary activities. And going by the activities of Paul in the book of Acts, it is clear that Christian missions indeed is God's own project.

CHAPTER ELEVEN

HOW WEALTHY ARE YOU?

Are you wealthy? You ought to be. You *must* be if you understand the Bible and flow with God's project. In this chapter, we shall examine two key scriptures:

> But you are to remember the Lord your God, for it is He who is giving you power to make wealth, in order to confirm His covenant which He swore to your fathers, as it is this day. (Deuteronomy 8:18)

> Consider the covenant; for the dark places of the land are full of the places of violence. (Psalm 74:20)

These passages talk of a covenant with which we ought to reckon and hold in regard.

But which covenant? I don't know if there is any other covenant with God in the Bible that is more prominent than the one with Abraham, the progenitor of Jesus the blessing (Genesis 12:1–3). This is widely referred to as the Abrahamic covenant.

By that covenant, the seed of Abraham is to be a blessing, or light, to the whole earth. It has been shown that God is more than committed to this. Our part is to be ready to key into any or all opportunities to participate in Christian missions.

Look through the Bible. Look around you. You will see that those who engage in the propagation of the gospel are usually wealthy. The extent to which you accumulate wealth is determined by the extent to which you give yourself to the business of propagating the gospel.

A second golden question is this: *why does God give this power to create wealth? The answer is that* He readily gave it for the purpose of establishing the Abrahamic covenant. Wherever there is no light, the works of darkness and violence abound. And what are the works of darkness? The wickedness of the devil.

I know a certain settlement in Nigeria to which Agape Missions, a Christian missions agency, sent a pioneering missionary in the early 1990s. Like with any other unreached community, this settlement lacked most amenities. They did their washing and drinking from a stream and used the vast surrounding bush for defecating.

In a place such as this, where there was no scrap of education, you can imagine how healthy the inhabitants were. A person would be very old to live to fifty or sixty years. A woman who had lost four children would not be pitied, for child mortality was very high. In fact, in this settlement a child was to be sacrificed to the earth annually in exchange for the people yielding a harvest. Here, an entire family would live inside the same thatched-roof hut, with the children able to see their own parents make love. By being exposed to this, promiscuity was the order of the day.

This is how the devil knows how to rule in a place where there is no light of the gospel! He would raise "lords" for such people in the form of herbal spiritualists who would, in loyalty to him, serve as healer, protector, and giver of powers as local gods. The devil would punish them in disguise and take them with him to hellfire at the end of the day.

Psalm 74:20 explains why the whole earth is begging for the blessing of God. Jesus is the light of the world—and whenever light shines, darkness disappears. John 1:5 says, *"And the Light shines in the darkness, and the darkness did not grasp it."* His coming to the world brought light wherever He went (Mark 9:35).

After emptying Himself on His followers, they became the light, since He had to vacate the scene (Matthew 5:14, 2 Corinthians 2:14). This is why His followers must take the light everywhere.

Why then wouldn't God create wealth for anyone who's ready to take His light to the world? Clearly, the power of God to create wealth for anyone is premised upon that person's readiness to do the business of establishing the Abrahamic covenant. How does He do this? He causes a person's land to yield an increase. He blesses whatever we set our hands upon!

Take it from me: the power to attain wealth is at your disposal. You don't have to pray and fast. Just take your cue from Jesus's prayer in Matthew 9:38: *"Pray ye therefore the Lord of the harvest, that he will send forth labourers into his harvest"* (KJV). That is the Master's heartfelt desire!

What is your own prayer request? It's no wonder that so many prayers go unanswered. I bet you that anyone whose desire for wealth is premised upon gospel purposes gets it. As the Bible says, *"And this is the confidence that we have in him, that, if we ask any thing according to his will, he heareth us"* (1 John 5:14, KJV).

On the other hand, according to James 4:3, *"Ye ask and, and receive not, because ye ask amiss, that ye may consume it upon your lusts"* (KJV).

Let your asking be in accordance with the Lord's will rather than your own lusts. Choose the lusts of the Lord. And what are His lusts? Luke 19:10 tells us that they are to seek and save the lost.

CONCLUSION

It is clear from looking at Matthew 24:14 and Mark 13:10 that the Lord expects the gospel to be preached in every nation before the end comes. So if you encounter any opportunity to organize, participate in, sponsor, or pursue a Christian activity, do it. The result will be the spreading of the gospel, even to the unreached places of the world.

My conclusion therefore is this: we must get over all our hindrances—ignorance, deception, shadow-chasing, laziness, indolence, sleepiness, sheepishness, and churchiness—and key into everything it takes to engage in missions in order to see God's truth reach the whole world. The truth is that Jesus is the way, the truth, and the life and there is no other name under heaven by which we can be saved.

Souls are perishing and time is running out!

ABOUT THE AUTHOR

Adewunmi Makanjuola holds a Bachelor of Laws (LL.B), Master of Law (LL.M), and Barrister-at-Law (B.L.). He was called to the Nigerian bar in 1990 and earned a diploma in pastoral studies from Victory Life Bible Schol in Ilesa, Nigeria in 2005.

With the mindset of having been saved to serve, and having been raised in an evangelistic milieu, he has pioneered soul-winning squads in Jos, Nigeria and later pastored a church near Ilesa. He remains engaged with missions and missionary activities.

He practiced law for ten years, magistracy for eighteen years, and retired as deputy chief registrar of the High Court of Justice in the Osun state of Nigeria. He is presently based in Manitoba, Canada. He is married to Princess Adetayo and has been blessed with amazing children.

www.ingramcontent.com/pod-product-compliance
Lightning Source LLC
Chambersburg PA
CBHW032020040426
42448CB00006B/683